Missile Defenses and American Security 2004

The International Dimension

American Foreign Policy Council

UNIVERSITY PRESS OF AMERICA,® INC.
Lanham • Boulder • New York • Toronto • Plymouth, UK

The American Foreign Policy Council is a private educational foundation established in 1982 to bring information to those who make or influence the policy of the United States, and to assist leaders in the former USSR and other parts of the world in building democracies and market economies.

The American Foreign Policy Council is incorporated in the District of Columbia, and is a tax-exempt organization under section 501(c)(3) of the United States Internal Revenue Code.

Copyright © 2008 by the American Foreign Policy Council.

All rights reserved. No part of this publication may be produced or transmitted in any form or by any means, electronic or mechanical, including photocopying, recording or any information storage and retrieval system, without permission in writing from the holder of the copyright.

American Foreign Policy Council
509 C Street, NE
Washington, D.C. 20002

Printed in the United States of America

University Press of America,® Inc.
4501 Forbes Boulevard
Suite 200
Lanham, Maryland 20706
UPA Acquisitions Department (301) 459-3366

Estover Road
Plymouth PL6 7PY
United Kingdom

British Library Cataloging in Publication Information Available

Copublished by arrangement with the American Foreign Policy Cuncil

Library of Congress Control Number: 2007942936
ISBN-13: 978-0-7618-3988-0 (paperback : alk. paper)
ISBN-10: 0-7618-3988-7 (paperback : alk. paper)

∞™ The paper used in this publication meets the minimum requirements of American National Standard for Information Sciences—Permanence of Paper for Printed Library Materials, ANSI Z39.48—1984

Contents

Introduction *Herman Pirchner, Jr.*	1
Keynote Address: America's Cooperative Approach to Missile Defense *The Honorable Stephen G. Rademaker*	3
Panel I: Allied Perspectives on Missile Defense	15
Missile Proliferation and Missile Threats in the Middle East *Uzi Rubin*	17
Missiles and Missile Defense in Europe *Radek Sikorski*	23
Canada's Role in Hemispheric Defense *Dr. James Fergusson*	27
Japan's Response to New Threats in Asia *Atsushi Ando*	33
Panel II: New Threats and Challenges	37
Collective Defense and Coalition Solidarity *David Trachtenberg*	39
Arresting Asymmetric Proliferation *Ilan Berman*	47

Introduction

Herman Pirchner, Jr.[1]

Things have changed significantly since the first conference on "Missile Defenses and American Security," which was convened a day after President Bush announced his decision to deploy a missile defense system to defend the American people against ballistic missile attack. Today, the long-running debate over whether to deploy such defenses largely has been settled. The only question that remains is what will be deployed, when and how.

The President has made clear that he is pursuing a broad missile defense program as opposed to an exclusive *national* missile defense system. In other words, the United States intends to protect not only itself, but also its allies throughout the world. With that in mind, this year's conference deals with two pressing issues. The first is international cooperation, and how the issue of how our allies will fit into America's emerging anti-missile effort— and how other nations could be included over time.

The second is emerging threats. When missile defenses first came to the forefront of the national security debate in the United States, at the height of the Cold War, it was easy to identify and adversary; the Soviet Union. With that conflict over, we have begun to think more and more about the threat from rogue states, terrorism and other asymmetric dangers.

The pages that follow provide insights from some of our country's leading experts about the future shape of American missile defense, and its future adversaries.

---

[1]Herman Pirchner is President of the American Foreign Policy Council.

Keynote Address: America's Cooperative Approach to Missile Defense

*The Honorable Stephen G. Rademaker**

All of us remember when missile defense was ridiculed. We were told it was a dangerous fantasy. The technology wouldn't work. It was too costly. It would trigger a new arms race. This last criticism was perhaps the most damning; it is what allegedly made missile defense not just a fantasy, but a dangerous fantasy.

Everyone agreed that we could not effectively defend America against the threat of missile attack while continuing to adhere to the Anti-Ballistic Missile Treaty of 1972. And, it was said, the ABM Treaty was all that stood between us and a new arms race, because that Treaty was the cornerstone of strategic stability. Without that cornerstone, the structure of arms control would collapse. Thus, the opponents of missile defense were able to argue that having missile defense interceptors—a weapon that can only defend people and not attack them—would not protect us, but rather would make us less secure.

And so the battle lines were drawn. Either you were for missile defense or you were for arms control and strategic stability, but you could not be for both, the critics claimed.

Of course, the intellectual underpinnings of this critique collapsed when the United States announced its withdrawal from the ABM Treaty in December of 2001. Far from triggering a new arms race, that announcement ushered in a new round of U.S.-Russian strategic arms control. Just five months later, in May of 2002, Presidents Bush and Putin signed the

---

*The Honorable Stephen G. Rademaker is Assistant Secretary for Arms Control, a post he has held since August 2002.

Moscow Treaty, which provided for a two-thirds reduction in the number of strategic nuclear warheads on each side. This was the deepest reduction ever mandated by a strategic arms control treaty. Equally telling, it was the first treaty reducing nuclear weapons to be signed by the United States and Russia in nine and a half years.

This is not to say that there were no efforts to negotiate a new treaty reducing nuclear weapons during the Clinton Administration, because clearly there were. But those efforts always foundered on the problem of how to preserve the ABM Treaty despite the fact that it was becoming increasingly obsolete. Indeed, that problem not only stopped the Clinton Administration from concluding a new treaty reducing nuclear weapons, but also prevented it from bringing into force the last such treaty negotiated by the United States, the START II Treaty of 1993 which had been signed during the final days of the Administration of President George H.W. Bush. So it can be said that by 2001, the ABM Treaty was not the cornerstone of strategic arms control, but rather a principal obstacle to progress in arms control.

In view of these developments, missile defense is no longer ridiculed the way it used to be. We still encounter plenty of strong opposition, but both the breadth and depth of that opposition is diminishing as people come to understand current strategic realities and the details of our policy. Increasingly, the need for missile defense is being recognized as self-evident, just as Schopenhauer might have predicted.

This is true not only within the United States, but overseas as well. Indeed, when it comes to foreign governments, which are the focus of my remarks today, I would say that, with very few exceptions, they fully accept the need to move forward with missile defense in the current security environment. Foreign publics are often a different matter, however. Not surprisingly, many people in foreign countries pay less attention to these matters than do the officials of their governments, just as is the case in our country. As a result, foreign publics often continue to accept the now disproven contention that we can have either missile defense on the one hand or arms control and strategic stability on the other, but not both. Still thinking that they need to choose between these two options, they instinctively express a preference for arms control and strategic stability.

This is a false dilemma, for reasons that I have already explained, and most foreign governments today understand that no such choice needs to be made. There can be little doubt that the understanding of foreign publics eventually will catch up with the understanding of foreign governments. Until it does, however, many of our potential partners overseas will be in a bit of a bind. They want to cooperate with us on missile defense because they know it is the right thing to do and because they recognize that it will enhance their security. At the same time, they need to proceed cautiously because public opinion has not yet fully absorbed current strategic realities, and like all democratic governments, they wish to minimize criticism, even ill founded criticism.

There can be little doubt about how this will play out over time. As the economists say, what really matters is the fundamentals, and the fundamentals all come down in favor of missile defense. First, there is the fact that arms control and strategic stability will not be weakened by missile defense. Second, the technology is now available, it is proving itself, notwithstanding the predictable setbacks from time to time, and the technology will only get better over time. Finally, there is the fact that the threat to all of us is growing.

Today, roughly two dozen countries, including some of the world's least responsible regimes, possess ballistic missiles, and many are attempting to obtain missiles of longer range. Many of these regimes also have nuclear, biological, or chemical weapons programs.

One of the key reasons potential adversaries seek ballistic missiles is because we have had no defense against long-range missiles, and only a limited defense against shorter-range missiles. Absent defenses, even older, unsophisticated ballistic missiles are capable of delivering devastating WMD attacks against population centers. Potential adversaries see these weapons as a means for exploiting an obvious vulnerability of ourselves and our friends and allies.

For example, North Korea continues to develop and deploy ballistic missiles of all ranges while also working to expand its nuclear capability. North Korea is nearly self-sufficient in developing and producing ballistic missiles, and it has been eager to sell complete missile systems or components to other countries. This in turn has enabled other countries to acquire longer-range capabilities earlier than would otherwise have been possible, while often establishing the basis for indigenous development and production efforts.

No Dong missile sales by North Korea have transformed the missile capabilities of some countries in just a few years. We also must worry about the direct threat from North Korean missiles. The vulnerability of our ally, Japan, to North Korean missiles was highlighted in August 1998 by the launch of the Taepo Dong 1 in a space launch vehicle, or SLV, configuration that flew over Japan to impact in the Pacific Ocean. North Korea continues to develop the more advanced Taepo Dong 2 ICBM/SLV, potentially capable of reaching the United States. This missile could be flight-tested at any time. If North Korea were to use a third stage on a Taepo Dong 2, as it did in the 1998 Taepo Dong 1 test, such a three stage missile could deliver a several hundred kilogram payload up to 15,000 kilometers. The missile also has sufficient range to target all of Europe.

Iran and Syria can currently reach the territory of U.S. friends and allies with their ballistic missiles. Iran's declared intent to develop the complete nuclear fuel cycle, combined with its history of concealing potentially weapons-related activities in violation of its nuclear safeguards agreement with the IAEA, leaves little doubt that Iran is seeking a nuclear weapons capability. Iran and other countries also are working on space launch vehicles, and SLVs contain most of the key building blocks for an ICBM. These systems could be ready for flight-testing in the middle to latter-part of the decade. Ballistic missiles from Iran can already reach some parts of Europe, and, of course, Iranian and Syrian ballistic missiles threaten our coalition forces deployed in the Middle East.

For these reasons, there is a growing risk that hostile states could deliver WMD by ballistic missiles to all parts of Europe within a decade. Further, if North Korea chooses to sell its longer-range ballistic missiles to customers in the Middle East—as it has done with its shorter-range systems—the risk to our friends and allies could grow exponentially. And it is important to recognize that the limited accuracy and targeting capabilities of emerging ballistic missile threats suggests that hostile states possessing such missiles likely would target the population and territory of our friends and allies rather than their military forces and facilities.

President George W. Bush recognized during his first presidential campaign that many of our friends and allies are no less threatened by missiles than are we. He further recognized that the integrity of the NATO Alliance could be diminished if the United States were protected against missile attack but our allies in Europe were not. Accordingly, he resolved to seek to ensure that our allies would also have protection against missile attack.

In NSPD-23, President Bush translated this commitment into U.S. Government policy. Promulgated on December 16, 2002, NSPD-23 states:

> *Because the threats of the 21st century also endanger our friends and allies around the world, it is essential that we work together to defend against them. The Defense Department will develop and deploy missile defenses capable of protecting not only the United States and our deployed forces, but also our friends and allies.*

NSPD-23 further directs the Department of Defense to:

> *... structure the missile defense program in a manner that encourages industrial participation by friends and allies, consistent with overall U.S. national security ... and also promote international missile defense cooperation, including within bilateral and alliance structures such as NATO.*

The Bush Administration has been enthusiastically carrying out this policy over the past several years.

The United States is working jointly with interested friends and allies to analyze each country's unique threat environment and its missile defense requirements for the future. The Department of State has played and continues to play an important diplomatic role in this effort, explaining to allies and friends how missile defense can enhance regional security and stability while encouraging their cooperation and participation.

Participation in the U.S. missile defense program and the level of protection afforded to allies and friends by our missile defense systems will be determined as our systems evolve and as appropriate political, technical, and financial arrangements are agreed. Close collaboration and participation in the U.S. missile defense program by foreign governments can not only provide them with insights into the direction and details of our program, but may also influence the program. Foreign government contributions might involve financial investments or "in-kind" contributions such as indigenous technologies, technical expertise, provision of targets, or affording the use of facilities or territory.

Additionally, depending upon the particulars, foreign government participation might also include foreign military sales or direct commercial sales of U.S. systems and co-development, co-production or licensed production of missile defense systems. Naturally, a foreign government's degree of insight and influence will be proportional to its contribution to the U.S. missile defense program.

The governments with which we are either carrying out or discussing missile defense cooperation include Japan, the United Kingdom, Denmark, Australia, Canada, Israel, The Netherlands, Germany, Italy, Russia, Turkey, Spain, Poland, the Czech Republic, Hungary, Ukraine, Taiwan, and India. With your indulgence, I will describe the particulars of our cooperation with some of these governments.

JAPAN

As I have already noted, Japan's vulnerability to North Korean missile attack was demonstrated dramatically in 1998 when North Korea launched a Taepo Dong missile, configured as a space launch vehicle over Japan. Not coincidentally, since 1999, Japan and the United States have worked side-by-side on missile defense. The United States and Japan expect to sign in the near future a Framework Memorandum of Understanding, or a Framework MoU, for short, that will further facilitate the extensive industrial cooperation already underway.

Since 1999, Japan has spent about $131 million in cooperative research with the United States on upgrades to the Standard Missile 3 (SM-3). The bulk of this work has focused on several key SM-3 components, including the nosecone, second-stage propulsion system, infrared sensor, and a divert and attitude control system for the advanced kinetic warhead.

Japan currently has 24 operational PAC-2 missile fire units (120 launchers) and four Aegis/SM-2 equipped destroyers. Japan's four AWACS aircraft and its existing ground based air defense command and control system provide other elements for building a missile defense architecture. On December 19, 2003, the Japanese government announced its plans to acquire and deploy the PAC-3 and Aegis/SM-3 and to achieve Initial Operational Capability for both systems by 2007 and Full Operational Capability by 2011. Japan's FY2004 defense budget of $42 billion includes $1 billion for missile defense. Of this total, $543 million will be allocated for a phased upgrade of all firing units in Japan with a mix of PAC-3 and the remainder PAC-2 GEM+. Another $320 million has been earmarked for upgrading one AEGIS destroyer and acquiring SM-3 missiles to equip it. Japan is also developing a new radar designed primarily for missile defense search and tracking. Continuing U.S.-Japan joint research will also be funded. In August, the Japanese Defense Agency requested $1.3 billion for missile defense for FY2005.

UNITED KINGDOM

British Defense Minister Hoon and Secretary of Defense Rumsfeld signed a Ballistic Missile Defense Cooperation Framework MoU, on June 12, 2003. This agreement establishes the basis for U.S.-U.K. industrial collaboration in the field of missile defense. An Annex to the Framework MoU regarding the Fylingdales early warning radar was signed on December 18, 2003, authorizing us to upgrade that radar for use in missile defense. These upgrades will allow the radar to generate the information necessary to direct a midcourse missile defense interceptor to the general area of the intercept. This event marked the first time a U.S. ally permitted deployment of a missile defense system component on its territory to assist us in defending U.S. territory.

Another Annex on Missile Defense Research, Development, Testing and Evaluation (RDT&E) cooperation was signed on October 12, 2004. To assist in both government-to-government, and industry-to-industry RDT&E cooperation in missile defense, the U.K. established its Missile Defence Centre in July 2003. The Centre attempts to bring U.K. government and industry expertise together by providing a centralized clearinghouse for the ultimate purpose of establishing closer technical and industrial cooperation.

DENMARK

In May 2004, the United States received the Danish government's agreement to permit upgrades to the U.S. early warning radar at Thule Air Base, Greenland. This upgrade will enhance our capability to detect and defend against ballistic missile attacks launched from the Middle East. We aim to complete the early warning radar upgrades at Thule in 2007. Negotiations for a bilateral Framework MoU to facilitate missile defense cooperation began in November 2004.

AUSTRALIA

On December 4, 2003, the Government of Australia announced its decision to participate in the U.S. missile defense program. Australian Minister of Defence Robert Hill said: "The Government is concerned that Australia might one day be threatened by long range missiles with mass destruction effect and believes that investment in defensive measures is important." According to Minister Hill's media release, Australia is "working with the U.S. to determine the most appropriate forms of Australian participation that will not only be in our strategic defence interests but also provide maximum opportunities for Australian industry." The United States and Australia signed a Framework MoU on missile defense cooperation on July 7th of this year, which will facilitate bilateral government-to-government and industry-to-industry cooperation. The United States and Australia are currently working to identify projects for future cooperation; potential areas include launch surveillance, detection, and tracking.

CANADA

On December 1, President Bush delivered a speech in Halifax, Nova Scotia, in which he expressed his hope that Canada will agree to bilateral missile defense cooperation in order to "protect the next generation of Canadians and Americans from the threats we know will arise." We exchanged diplomatic notes with Canada on August 5, 2004, to amend the NORAD Agreement in order to permit NORAD to provide Integrated Tactical Warning/Attack Assessment in support of USNORTHCOM's execution of the missile defense mission. This agreement does not commit Canada to participate in our missile defense system. The fundamental principles guiding the direction of U.S.-Canada missile defense cooperation were spelled out in an exchange of letters between the Secretary of Defense and the Minister of National Defence on January 15, 2004, which was publicly released.

ISRAEL

In order to assist Israel in responding to the threats emanating from other Middle Eastern countries, the United States has been helping Israel develop and field missile defense capabilities. Apart from providing Patriot batteries to Israel, we have since 1988 cooperated on, and jointly funded, the development of Israel's Arrow missile defense system. The first Arrow battery was fielded near Tel Aviv and became fully operational in October 2002.

Today, we are continuing to assist Israel in the Arrow System Improvement Program. Elements of this program include performance upgrades to the operational system in order to give the system greater capability against longer-range threats of greater sophistication, testing the Arrow system at a U.S. test range, assisting Israel in the procurement of a third Arrow battery, and co-producing the interceptor. As part of the cooperative joint testing project, this past summer Israel conducted two flight tests of the Arrow from Point Magu, California. Unlike the Israeli test range, with its range safety restrictions, Point Magu permits testing against a real-world SCUD.

INDIA

On January 12th of this year, President Bush and then-Prime Minister Vajpayee announced the "Next Steps in Strategic Partnership" ("NSSP") initiative. This initiative includes a strategic stability dialogue with India, including an expanding discussion of missile defense. The United States and India have also conducted joint missile defense workshops.

North Atlantic Treaty Organization

NATO has been working on missile defense for a number of years. Prior to the Prague Summit in November 2002, NATO Allies agreed on the need for theater missile defenses to protect deployed Alliance forces against shorter-range missile threats. Active Layered Ballistic Missile Defense feasibility studies for deploying missile defenses capable of protecting Allied military forces were initiated in June 2001 and completed in January 2003. Drawing on the results of these studies, NATO developed a basic acquisition strategy for missile defense of deployed Alliance forces. The Alliance is now in the process of implementing that strategy, and contracts for missile defense equipment and infrastructure will begin to be awarded starting in 2006.

At the Prague Summit, NATO agreed to examine options for addressing the increasing ballistic missile threat to not only Alliance forces, but also Alliance territory and population centers. Consequently, two studies were undertaken—one to assess the longer-term threat to NATO territory from ballistic missiles and another to examine ways to protect Alliance populations and territory from the ballistic missile threat. The first study on the longer-term threat to NATO was presented to Foreign Ministers at the December 8, 2004 meeting of the North Atlantic Council. The second report on the feasibility of protecting Alliance territory and population centers is due in July 2005.

At the Istanbul Summit in June 2004, Heads of State and Government endorsed the Alliance's work on ballistic missile defense. In addition, they agreed that a tri-national Extended Air Defense Task Force would be used as a military resource to begin integrating missile defense capabilities into the Alliance. Heads of State and Government also directed that work on ballistic missile defense be moved forward expeditiously.

NETHERLANDS AND GERMANY

The Netherlands, Germany, and the United States are examining Extended Air Defense/Theater Missile Defense integration and interoperability through the Dutch-hosted Project Optic Windmill Joint Exercise and the U.S.-hosted Roving Sands Exercise.

MEADS: U.S., GERMANY, AND ITALY

The governments of Germany, Italy, and the United States have been pursuing a multilateral research and development program to field a new mobile air and missile defense system capable of providing protection for forces on the move called the Medium Extended Air Defense System (MEADS). MEADS is expected to replace the U.S. Army's Patriot system in the next decade and has the potential to become the core short-range missile defense capability for the Alliance.

Italy recently signed a memorandum of understanding with the U.S. in September 2004. Both Germany and Italy support MEADS and have programmed funding for the next phase of activities. Germany, in spite of national fiscal constraints, is projected to spend about $1.4 billion to field 12-24 MEADS units.

THIRD SITE EXPLORATORY TALKS

Consistent with the President's policy direction, we have been examining options for enhancing both the defenses of the United States and of our allies and friends by deploying additional long-range ground-based interceptors, additional sensors, and possibly establishing additional sites for ground-based interceptor launchers and forward-based radars. One option would involve deploying a U.S. missile defense interceptor site in Europe. Such a site in Europe has the advantage that it could both defend much of

Europe and supplement our capability to defend the United States. U.S. system components deployed in Europe and in states adjacent to Middle East threats would fulfill the President's objective of making sure that both we and our friends and allies in Europe have some protection against intermediate-range threats from the Middle East as well as long-range threats from North Korea.

I would emphasize that despite our on-going consultations with a number of countries, including Poland, our talks are still exploratory. No decision has been made regarding the deployment of a third ground-based missile defense launcher site, much less whether it will be located in the United States or in Europe. U.S. officials have conducted exploratory and preliminary consultations with a number of countries in Europe who have expressed interest in potentially hosting such a site, and it is our hope that these discussions will continue.

The limited numbers of interceptors to be deployed in the United States and potentially at a third site in Europe demonstrates that our missile defense system is limited in nature and is directed against attacks by rogue states. It is not directed against the Russian Federation, and even with the addition of a third site in Europe it would not undermine Russia's deterrent. I and other officials of the U.S. Government have been keeping the Russian Government informed about our talks to potentially establish a third interceptor site in Europe, and we will continue to do so.

U.S.-RUSSIA

Under the May 24, 2002, Presidential Joint Declaration signed at the Moscow Summit, the United States and Russia "agreed to implement a number of steps aimed at strengthening confidence and increasing transparency in the area of missile defense," including information exchanges, visits, exhibitions, and observation of flight-tests. The Missile Defense Working Group—also referred to as Working Group #2—is the key U.S.-Russian forum for discussing bilateral missile defense cooperation, as well as for implementing measures to increase transparency and strengthen confidence in the missile defense field. Working Group #2 was established under the auspices of the Consultative Group for Strategic Security on September 20, 2002. The United States has provided comprehensive briefings and programmatic status updates at every meeting. Additionally, the U.S. has offered on a voluntary and reciprocal basis to host visits to U.S. missile defense sites, including visits to observe missile defense-related flight-tests, and to exhibit missile defense systems.

We want missile defense cooperation to be an important part of the new relationship the United States and Russia are building for the 21st century.

The 2002 Joint Declaration committed both sides to explore "potential programs for the joint research and development of missile defense technologies." Despite the June 1, 2003, St. Petersburg Joint Statement endorsing greater bilateral cooperation in the field of missile defense, progress has been extremely slow. Nevertheless, U.S. and Russian experts are currently negotiating a Defense Technical Cooperation Agreement (an agreement somewhat similar to the Framework MoUs either completed or under negotiation with our friends and allies), which would facilitate both government-to-government, as well as, industry-to-industry cooperation in the missile defense field. At the September 2003 Camp David Summit, Presidents Bush and Putin agreed that missile defense cooperation should be an important part of our bilateral cooperation and put it on their Action Checklist. That was re-affirmed at their meeting on June 8th of this year at Sea Island, Georgia, on the margins of the G-8 Summit.

NATO-RUSSIA

NATO has also been pursuing missile defense cooperation with Russia. At the Rome Summit of 2002, NATO and Russia committed to explore cooperation in theater missile defense, or TMD. This work is done under the Ad Hoc Working Group on Theater Missile Defense of the NATO-Russia Council. This working group has developed several preliminary products, including common terminology, and the development of TMD experimental concepts.

The focus of this work is to develop and implement a concept of operations that would allow effective use of both NATO and Russian missile defense systems in any future crisis where both were working together outside of NATO territory—in other words, in a non-Article V operation. A NATO-Russia Command Post Exercise was held in March 2004 at the Joint National Integration Center in Colorado Springs to test elements of the experimental concept of operations; another is planned for 2005.

INDUSTRY-TO-INDUSTRY COOPERATION

So far I have only discussed part of the equation. Before I leave you with the impression that only government-to-government cooperation is possible in the field of missile defense, let me quickly list just a few examples of how American industry is cooperating independently with industry in Europe, Asia, and Australia on a broad range of missile defense R&D projects.

Lockheed Martin, for instance, and BAE Systems in the United Kingdom have signed an MoU to explore partnership opportunities on missile defense programs around the world. This agreement envisions joint investments in key technologies that can significantly enhance the effectiveness of sea-based systems, systems integration, command and control, early warning and sensor networking, interceptors, use of targets, and dealing with countermeasures. This international team is working to expand transatlantic missile defense cooperation for the benefit of both the United States and NATO Allies by leveraging the best technologies and engineering skills each company and each nation has to offer.

Lockheed Martin has also signed an MoU with Poland's leading defense electronics company, PIT. This agreement paves the way for the two companies to explore opportunities for missile defense cooperation and gives PIT access to new markets and technology that will further industrial cooperation between the United States and Poland.

Boeing has signed an MoU with European weapons manufacturer MBDA to evaluate and develop short-term and long-term business relationships that will examine architectures for defending against global and regional ballistic missile threats.

Boeing has also announced a missile defense partnership with CEA Technologies of Australia to pursue joint research and development of missile defense technologies. We hope that U.S. and Russian enterprises will develop similar industrial relationships as soon as possible— even prior to the signing of a bilateral Defense Technical Cooperation Agreement between the United States and the Russian Federation.

CONCLUSION

The National Security Strategy of the United States clearly states that we are "guided by the conviction that no nation can build a safer, better world alone." This philosophy guides our approach to the full array of national security challenges before us, including the challenge of deploying effective missile defenses.

I hope the examples I have given make clear that our interest in cooperating with friends and allies is being reciprocated. The number of countries with which we are cooperating on missile defense is continuing to grow, as is the intensity of that cooperation, and this promises to greatly enhance the security of us all.

I
ALLIED PERSPECTIVES ON MISSILE DEFENSE

Missile Proliferation and Missile Threats in the Middle East

Uzi Rubin*

I am here today to talk about missile proliferation from the Israeli perspective. However, I must stress that I am speaking as a private citizen, and do not represent the official views or policies of the Israeli government.

What I am going to speak about today is truly open source. As we know, open source has a poor "noise to signal ratio," so what I have tried to do is sift through all the "noise" and bring forth the facts and trends that I think are most plausible. And, although what is plausible is usually not too far from the truth, I ask you not to take this as a confirmed intelligence-level view of proliferation in the Middle East. Nevertheless, here is missile proliferation in the Middle East at a glance:

Material comes from three sources: North Korea, China, and Russia. With regard to proliferation from North Korea, there is actually a bit of controversy. Some researchers have maintained that the real source of material is not North Korea, but Russia, and that North Korea is just a way-station. According to this view, it is actually Russian technology and Russian equipment that is being transferred through North Korea. There are also very convincing arguments why this in fact is not the case. So let me just say that the jury is out, and leave it at that. In China, we see a country that is a supplier primarily of materials and goods, but not necessarily of complete missiles. China has applied for membership in the Missile Technology Control

---

[1]Uzi Rubin is President of Rubincon Defense Consulting in Israel. Mr. Rubin established the Israeli Missile Defense Organization in January of 1991, and headed it until July of 1999. During that period, he was in charge of Israel's Arrow Missile Defense Program and led it from initial design through full scale development and testing to a series of manufacturing and eventually to operational deployment.

Regime (MTCR) but was turned down. In response, it has enacted its own MTCR. I have researched it very carefully, and it looks very much like the American MTCR, although it is missing several key items. From these omissions you can see that the Chinese allow themselves to export certain technologies—GPS systems, for instance. As for Russia, it is not clear whether material is coming directly from Russia or from Russian entities or even from rogue operations. Some private talks I have had with Russian political analysts revealed a lot of resistance to arming Iran. But again, it is not clear whether there is a hidden Russian agenda in supporting the Iranians or maybe it is out of their control. Again, the jury is out.

Regional states are engaged in secondary proliferation. Iran is both a recipient and a distributor of proliferated weapons. Indeed, secondary proliferation is very common among states like Syria and Lebanon, which are receiving material from Iran, Pakistan, and Saudi Arabia.

Technology components continue to flow in, missiles are becoming more advanced and stockpiles are rising at a moderate rate. Local cruise missiles have made their first appearance. Of course, cruise missiles were used by the United States copiously in both Gulf Wars, but during Operation Iraqi Freedom we saw for the first time the use of Iraqi cruise missiles against Coalition forces. Likewise, we have recently seen the appearance of locally made UAVs; Iranian made UAVs, for instance, have been confirmed over Israel.

Who are the major players? First, let us remember that two players are out of the game; Iraq and Libya are no longer proliferation threats. Iraq was forcefully disarmed, Libya willingly so. Libya is a mystery as far as intentions go. I would expect them to try to get ballistic missiles with a 1,000 kilometer range, because that would bring Israel into the picture. But according to open source reports, Libya has been engaged in developing 800 km ballistic missiles. This range does not make sense. I therefore judge the information to be not too reliable. Libya also has requested membership in the MTCR, which I found ironic enough to mention here.

More important than Libya is Iraq. As you know, Iraq operated and fired its own 180 kilometer-range *Fatah* and *Samoud* missiles. We know that the *Fatah* is a solid propellant unguided rocket, which was receiving improvements in accuracy. The *Samoud* is a liquid propellant missile based on the SA-2, a Russian anti-aircraft missile. Iraq bought about 500 such engines from Poland, and they based this missile on that design. Both missiles were fired at American forces in Kuwait and in Iraq, and similar weapons were intercepted and shot down by PAC-2s and PAC-3s. Iraq also operated and fired its own cruise missiles based on the Chinese *Silkworm* design. British forces captured the Iraqi version of the *Silkworm* in Basra.

Iraq's ultimate goal was to break out of sanctions, gain access to international markets and thereby restart a complete missile program. Saddam had ordered the initiation of a program for the development of a 1,000 kilometer land attack cruise missile named the *Jenin*. More important for Saddam was his ability to preserve human capital. Missiles are high tech; you can take away the machinery, but you must keep the people. And remarkably, despite the sanctions, Saddam had managed to keep the human resources intact. Thus, an Iraqi missile program could have conceivably broken out again. But now, let's move on to the active players.

Yemen is a God-forsaken country stuck somewhere in the Arabian Peninsula. But it does have missiles. It made headlines prior to the start of Operation Iraqi Freedom, when a missile shipment from North Korea was stopped in the Indian Ocean, and then released. Yemen keeps a low profile with its missile program, with no public displays and no testing.

Egypt, according to open sources, has maintained a large arsenal of ballistic missiles, both *Scud Bs* and *Scud Cs*. The latter missile can reach Israel from the Nile Delta. Reportedly, the Egyptians were trying to buy *No Dong* missiles from North Korea, but were discouraged from doing so by the United States. Since the late 1980s, and the exit of their then-Minister of Defense, Abu Ghazala, the Egyptians have been playing down their missile force as much as they can. Their capability remains very, very local; no public displays. And I have never heard of Egypt testing any missile.

Saudi Arabia still maintains anywhere between 30 and 60 CSS-2 missiles, although this capability is disputed. There were also strong rumors recently that Saudi Arabia was trying to expand its missile stockpile through purchases from either North Korea or Pakistan (more likely the latter). Today, you really don't hear anything about that anymore. Perhaps—and here I'm making a guess—this is a case of the "AQ Khan syndrome." Once the activities of the AQ Khan cartel became public, everybody became very, very cautious, and Saudi Arabia was forced to halt its efforts. Saudi Arabia, like Yemen and Egypt, keeps a low profile. There is no display, very few public references, no testing. I have never heard about any testing of Saudi owned missiles from Saudi Arabia.

Syria has a large arsenal of obsolete SS-21s, Scud Bs, and Scud Cs. It is currently producing both the Scud C and the Scud D. It supplied its own long-range unguided rockets to Lebanon and Hezbollah. For me, Hezbollah is synonymous with Syria and Iran. The Syrians have never publicly acknowledged having missiles, and have even gone so far as to deny it. But they test from time to time. The last known test was conducted back in 2001. Their arsenal is slowly growing, and it has been reported that they have chemical warheads on some of those Scuds.

Lebanon has several varieties of missiles, including the *Fajr 3* and *Fajr 5*, the latter of which can reach Israel, all the way down south of Haifa, from the Lebanese border. Their policy is very open. The leader of Hezbollah has made public statements that under certain conditions he will attack Israel with missiles and/or attack its major cities. So that is their stated policy.

Next are *Palestinian factions*. Some are making their own missiles and rockets. They are making both long-range and short-range variants. And they have started to utilize these domestically-produced rockets in attacks on Israel. These factions, moreover, have stated that they are increasing the range of these missiles, so the potential for destabilization is very grave.

Let's now turn to *Iran*. It has a stockpile of Scud Bs and Scud Cs, although they no longer produce them domestically. Iran fired Scud Bs into Iraq during the Iran-Iraq War. Before Operation Iraqi Freedom, it was very well advertised that hundreds of Scud Bs were fired at *mujahideen* bases in Iraq.

Iran acquired *No-Dong* missiles from North Korea and called it the *Shihab 3*. But then it surprised the world by firing a new and improved *Shihab* on August 11, 2004. This is what we call the *Shihab 3B*, or the *Shihab 4*. It has a range of 2,000 kilometers and although it is not an entirely new missile, it is amazingly adapted and dynamic. First, it's bigger and has a longer range. Second, the re-entry vehicle is completely different; it's more capable. Third, it has some fingerprints of Russian engineering; if you examine the design features of the new *Shihab* and then those of Soviet missiles, you see a lot of similarities. The *Shihab 4*'s instruments are smaller and system engineering is very good. This missile was clearly designed by proficient ballistic missile engineers. My personal feeling is that we are facing a world level team here.

Tellingly, as soon as international observers began discussing the *Shihab*'s similarities to Russian models, Iran stopped publicly showing missile launches. They fired a missile in October 2004 and broadcast some footage, but the footage was actually from 1999. We know from open sources that the missile they launched was the *Shihab 4*, yet their broadcast showed an older *Shihab 3*. Apparently, they got scared, and are trying to avoid some controversy.

Iran also has disclosed another family of relatively short range yet highly accurate ballistic missiles: the *Fatah 110*. It is essentially a bombardment rocket that Iran has turned into a ballistic missile with a range of about 250 kilometers. They are very proud of that; Iranian officials brag about this missile a lot, saying that they want to improve its accuracy even further.

Iran also recently announced that it would be beginning a space program. Its satellite launcher will be based on the *Shihab 3*. According to the calculations of Western experts, this launcher will be capable of orbiting only miniscule satellites. The program is in its infancy, however. A contract has been signed between the Iranian space industry and an Italian company called Calo Gavazzi to make a technological satellite called the *Masbeh*. There was another reference from the same source describing another product: a 170 kilogram-weight cartography and surveillance satellite.

This begs the question: why are they making satellite launchers that are only able to launch tiny weights, yet on the other hand making big heavy satellites to be launched by Russia? This is an indication that these two efforts are going to be melded together one day. That means we should expect a bigger Russian-Iranian satellite launcher in the future.

As we have seen above, Iran did develop a 2,000 kilometer-range missile—a weapon that it pledged in 2002 not to make. In fact, they are now bragging that they have it, and have boasted they can make a missile capable of traveling even further than that. Iranian officials deny vehemently that they are developing a 4,000 kilometer-range missile. But, based on their record of broken pledges, in all likelihood the next missile we see from Iran will indeed have a range of 4,000 kilometers, which would cover all of Europe. If I were a European, I would be very concerned about that.

Iran's actions, although disturbing enough in their own right, provide a strong motivation for other countries like Egypt to follow suit. They are also a very strong motivation for Saudi Arabia to arm itself in response, since Iran represents a mortal danger to the Saudi regime.

Finally, once the Iranians put their own satellite in space, they will be able see what's happening behind enemy lines. This represents an incredible tactical capability that's going to affect the balance of power within the Middle East and the balance of power between Iran and the rest of the world.

Missiles and Missile Defense in Europe

Radek Sikorski[1]

I have been asked to talk about the political ramifications of a missile launch station being based in Central Europe. And I have good news and bad news.

The good news is that Central Europeans feel comfortable with American leadership, both in general and with regard to specific defense issues. They perceive ballistic missiles to be a growing threat in international relations, although not necessarily to Central Europe.

Although this may be false consciousness, as Marxists used to put it, the people in Central Europe simply do not feel like important players in the Middle East drama. So, in the context of larger geopolitical calculations, they do not feel expressly threatened by ballistic missiles.

Yet they still wish to cooperate with the United States in defense matters because, I believe, an increasingly authoritarian Russia in the East is a threat they know all too well and are reluctant to face again.

America's reputation in the region has been greatly improved in the wake of the Ukrainian election scandal, because the United States, operating through Senator Lugar, President Bush, and Secretary Powell, worked in concert with the European Union to thwart this attempt to steal an election. This demonstrated that when we act together, we usually achieve success. Central Europe's faith in the United States and its appreciation of continued American interest in the region has been greatly fortified.

---

[1]Radek Sikorski is the Executive Director of the New Atlantic Initiative and a Resident Fellow at the American Enterprise Institute in Washington. He served as Poland's Deputy Minister of Foreign Affairs from 1998 to 2001. For Mr. Sikorski's latest views on Missile Defense, see his Washington Post Op-Ed; *Don't Take Poland For Granted* Wednesday, March 21, 2007; Page A15.

In general, Central Europeans believe that it is good to have missile defense, even if it is not likely to directly protect our region. Because if the system is located within our territory, the United States is much more likely to come to our assistance to protect it—thereby granting increased security to the whole region.

The bad news is that most countries in the region have become increasingly disillusioned with their involvement in the war in Iraq. As you may have heard, Hungary has decided to withdraw its troops by the end of this month, and Poland has just decided to reduce the size of its contingent from 2,500 to 1,700 troops next year.

The European public was in favor of getting involved in the operation to rid Iraq of Saddam Hussein because in a confrontation between the United States and Saddam, the United States is going to win, and it is better to support the winning side. People believed that the war would be quick, cheap, and an easy victory. But it is not exactly turning out that way.

The price for involvement in Iraq is now perceived to be too high, both politically and economically. Politically because these countries are new members of the European Union and it is well known that the "heavy hitters"—France and Germany—are opposed to the war. It is also suspected that these countries decided to back the European Constitution to diminish the influence of the war-supporting countries in Central Europe. The new Constitution would get away from the Nice Treaty provisions, which, for example, give Poland 27 votes in the Council of Ministers and thereby put Poland in a club of six powerful countries. The system of voting proposed by the European Constitution, however, would double the power of Germany and dilute the power, and thereby the influence, of Poland.

This was a very high price to pay, on top of the approximately $200 million per annum that Poland is paying for transporting and feeding troops in Iraq. This $200 million means that Poland has had to reduce programs aimed at modernizing its military forces to make them more compatible with NATO. And in return for this sacrifice, Poland feels no more secure as a result of Iraq. In fact, in some ways, we have lost security. We would never have even been on the radar screen of Al Qaeda, yet now we have had the dubious distinction of actually being mentioned by Osama bin Laden, Zarqawi and others in their various threats. That, of course, makes people very, very nervous.

So, for Central Europe, Iraq is not perceived to be a good investment. People do not feel good about being involved in a war that is dragging on; a war in which so many of our own soldiers are dying. Nor have Central European nations enjoyed the expected economic benefits from preferential treatment in the repayment of Iraqi debts, or from an inside track on rebuilding contracts. One of the most often used words in commentary on Polish-American relations of late is "asymmetry." This concept is perhaps best captured by a joke that I recently heard in the Polish parliament: "We buy F-16s, and in return we can send troops to Iraq."

Now, if an interceptor station is installed, the timeframe in which a decision must be made as to whether or not a missile that is being tracked must be intercepted is very small. Nor would this be a large base, like those of NATO in the past. It would require minimal staff, which lowers the potential economic benefits. And the host nation would not just be leasing the property, but essentially ceding territory and influence as well, including the sovereign power to launch violence at another country, to affect the strategic calculus of another country.

To obtain all this, the U.S. must think seriously about the kind of package that will have to be offered. Senior Pentagon representatives that I spoke with recently mentioned the possibility of a long-term contract for trash collection from the base as means of compensation. Quite frankly I don't think this will be satisfactory.

Given the current atmosphere in Central Europe this will be a difficult sell for the United States—particularly in the coming year, which is an election year for Poland. It is certain that both Iraq and missile defense will be frequent, and controversial, subjects.

In conclusion, I think missile defense is an opportunity to grow into an extra sinew of NATO. But if Central Europe is to be involved, we need more work to see what kind of package, what kind of scientific and industrial cooperation, will be needed to bridge the gap.

I think this point can be reached in five to ten years. In five to ten years, these countries will be able to finance their own expeditionary forces in the field with the United States. I believe the solidarity fund that has been mentioned in some quarters to reward those allies who have actually made a contribution, rather than those countries that are merely formal allies, will certainly help to make a Central European interceptor station into a reality.

Canada's Role in Hemispheric Defense

Dr. James Fergusson[1]

If I had stood in front of you a year ago, I would have had a very positive message for you about Canada. Today, however, it is an entirely different story.

Many of my colleagues in Canada would argue that if there is one classic textbook example of how a government should not handle an issue, it is the way Canada has handled the issue of missile defense. This does not just apply to the current minority government of Paul Martin. In fact, it predates Paul Martin. One could probably argue that it has been mishandled for not just one, but two or three decades, going right back to the 1960s—when Canada first confronted the issue of missile defense with regard to the Sentinel ABM system in 1967.

To understand Canada, you must realize that among America's allies, Canada is in a unique situation simply because of geography: we share a continent. But it is more than just geography. It is also a function of fundamentally common cultures, common values, and relatively common interests.

There are three key elements one always has to keep in mind when one talks about Canada and its bilateral defense relationship with the United States. The first is that Canada occupies a singular role in an institutionalized, integrated common command arrangement through the North American Aerospace Defense Command (NORAD). The importance of this relationship has always transcended common functional requirements of

---

[1] James Fergusson is a Senior Research Fellow of the Canadian Defense and Foreign Affairs Institute, as well as an Associate Professor at the University of Manitoba, where he teaches a range of courses in the areas of international relations, strategic studies, and foreign and defense policy.

defense during the Cold War and after. Rather, that relationship, that unique privilege, gave Canada insight into a much larger world than it would ever have been able to acquire on its own. It gave us a strategic picture of the aerospace nuclear dimension, something that most evidence indicates no other ally shared. Behind Canadian thinking about missile defense has been the issue of this privileged access, and how Canadian participation or nonparticipation will affect it.

Second is the simple fact that the system under consideration, the Ground-based Midcourse missile defense system now under deployment in Fort Greeley, Alaska, Vandenberg Air Force Base, and beyond, will defend Canada whether we like it or not. Regardless of what we do, Canada will be covered. This is not a new situation. It dates back to at least 1938 and Franklin Roosevelt's extension of a U.S. security umbrella over Canada, which has continued and has been institutionalized formally through NORAD. The result, however, is the belief that the United States will always defend Canada—and a priority on making sure that the U.S. defends us the way we want to be defended, rather than the way in which the United States would choose to do so alone. And, of course, this included a desire to maintain this relationship without having to pay very much for it.

The third element, and one that has been with us since at least the 1960s, is Canada's relationship with the United States as a function of its place in the world. Simply put, any issue that emerges on defense in this context turns into a political issue about Canadian sovereignty, about independence, and about identity. Once these issues have been raised, the Canadian government becomes extremely nervous, and we end up discussing not defense *per se*, but whether the issue in question makes us a satellite of the United States.

In the current debate, this involves the idea of Canadian prestige, and the risk that Canada's role on the international stage will be impaired if we cooperate with the United States on missile defense for continental North America. The end result is rhetoric of arm's-length distance that is constantly emphasized by Canadian decision-makers across the board, obscuring the simple reality of Canada's national interest in a close working relationship in the areas covered by missile defense.

Briefly, let me tell you where Canada stands right now. Canada has agreed to an initiative to have the early warning functions for the ground-based defenses being deployed in Alaska and California embedded in NORAD. This, however, is nothing new; Canada played a similar role for the U.S. Safeguard system in the 1970s. But it was a significant step for Canada in terms of protecting its interests in NORAD.

That was not, however, the real missile defense decision. When the Prime Minister made it clear that there was a decision on participation pending, it showed the problem with how this has typically been handled by the government. In his interview earlier this week, Mr. Martin said there would be no interceptors on Canadian soil. But, as far as I know, no one has asked Canada to put interceptors on Canadian soil. In fact, anyone who talks about the possibility of such a scenario is invariably Canadian. There is certainly no evidence to support the idea that the United States is somehow forcing us behind closed doors to consider these things.

Second, Mr. Martin said that Canada would not spend millions of dollars on participating in missile defense. The Prime Minister did not say that he wouldn't spend *any* money, but his refusal to spend millions is certainly not a surprise given the state of defense spending in the country, the rundown state of the Canadian armed forces and the billions of dollars needed simply to keep them alive. Certainly there is not going to be any significant money for missile defense coming from Canada.

Mr. Martin also declared that Canada would not support weapons in space. That is, of course, the traditional Canadian mantra, but weapons in space is an issue that is decades down the road; it is irrelevant, but certainly reflects the state of the domestic debate in Canada.

But the most interesting thing was what the Prime Minister has repeatedly noted; the United States has an obligation to consult with Canada and to allow Canadian input into the operational planning of the missile defense system for North America. I quote the Prime Minister: "If there is going to be an American missile going off over Canadian airspace, I think Canada should be at the table making the decision, and this becomes the key around the issue of what participation is."

In that regard, the politics of missile defense also stems from the unfortunate remarks made by President George W. Bush during his recent visit to Canada, which were interpreted as an implicit threat from the Americans that we had better get on board. Regardless of intent, the way in which the issue was raised reinforced the image in Canadian politics that the Bush administration considered Canadian participation a loyalty test.

How did we get to where we are today, with Canada keeping the United States at arm's length? Well, we can go back a long way, but the opening of the door to Canadian participation harkens back to the 1994 White Paper in which the Canadian government said that it was now interested in cooperation, consultation, and possibly participation, as well as a contribution in the area of surveillance and reconnaissance. But as national missile defense emerged and started to gain steam, Canadian policy shifted to what I call the three "nos." There is "no invitation." There is "no deployment decision." There is "no architecture." Hence, there is nothing for Canada to decide. The fundamental reason for the three "nos" was the perception in foreign affairs and defense circles that the issue was deeply divisive, especially within the Liberal caucus, and no one could predict which way the government might go. Hence it was better to leave it alone as long as possible.

This all began to change in 2003, which I would characterize as a period of moving towards full participation. In a speech to the Canadian Newspaper Association on April 30, 2003, Paul Martin—then just an ex-cabinet minister and member of parliament—said bluntly that he supported Canadian participation in missile defense. A month later, what is now the Conservative Party sponsored a motion in favor of Canadian participation through NORAD, which passed in the House of Commons by a vote of 156 to 73. Interestingly enough, the majority of liberals supported the motion, including the cabinet, with only 38 voting against the motion. In February 2004, another motion opposing participation was defeated, roughly by the same margin.

In June 2003, the Prime Minister announced discussions with the United States on Canadian participation. By that October, those discussions had actually yielded the outlines of a deal. Then, in December, when Paul Martin took over as Prime Minister, he made it clear that his fundamental foreign policy goal was to improve relations with the United States, which had been seriously damaged as a result of a variety of factors, including Canada's handling of the war in Iraq. Missile defense was potentially seen as one of the keys to improving relations.

Then we come to the remarkable letter sent by Defense Minister Pratt to the Pentagon in January 2004, which says that, "in light of the growing threat involving the proliferation of ballistic missiles and weapons of mass destruction, we should explore this partnership to include cooperation in missile defense." The letter references NORAD "as an appropriate response to these new threats and as a useful complement to our nonproliferation efforts."

Pratt went on to argue in favor of developing a bilateral, mutually-beneficial framework of understanding on missile defense: "We understand also that the United States is prepared to consult with Canada on operational planning issues associated with the defense of North America, and I propose that our staffs work together over the coming months to identify opportunities and mechanisms for such consultations and Canada's contribution."

By March–April, however, everything had come to a full stop, by and large because of declining Liberal popularity, particularly driven by the ad scandal in Canada, which many of you may not be familiar with. By the time we got into the election period (May–June), with the Liberals apparently headed for defeat by the last weeks of the campaign, Paul Martin draped himself in a nationalist flag. Liberals stated clearly that only the Liberal Party and Paul Martin can defend Canadian values, while the values of the Conservatives, which are U.S. values, would be stopped at the border.

Martin's nationalist turn proved successful in allowing him to at least salvage a minority government, and this became interpreted within senior circles as an important future issue for Canadian politics. And for that new minority leadership, missile defense is now seen as a political liability that could bring down the government, even though the reality is quite the opposite.

This leaves us with a divided Liberal Party, but also a newly-wavering Conservative Party which ironically decided after the election to withhold its views on missile defense until the government placed a formal proposal on the table. All in all, it represented a strange political situation, reflecting public opinion at the time.

Until 2003, the Canadian public was widely supportive of Canadian participation in missile defense. A poll done on the issue in 2000, for example, showed 76 percent of the Canadian population supporting involvement, and 82 percent agreeing that Canada-U.S. defense relations were of vital significance for Canada. Those levels are not surprising. NORAD has consistently garnered widespread support—from mid-70 to low 80 percent—in Canadian public opinion. By September 2004, however, public opinion had shifted significantly and Canada was split. 49 percent were against missile defense cooperation, and 44 in favor, with interesting differences depending on the region of the country surveyed.

What does this mean? First of all, the nation is divided on missile defense. But that division is by and large a function of the fact that many people associate missile defense with George W. Bush—and George W. Bush is not popular in Canada.

There was also a fear of political punishment; rather bizarre in the Canadian case because governments in Canada do not get punished on defense. Rather, politics in Canada are driven by very parochial domestic interests, with Medicare, social spending, and national unity at the top of the agenda. Only when framed through the sovereignty issue does defense begin to resonate, although even then not significantly.

Third, there has been a failure on the part of the government to actually put its case forward, allowing the opposition the opportunity to define the rules of the political fight. The government has not defended participation at all. It has basically responded to what the opposition parties and the anti-missile defense advocates have had to say about it. This inactivity on the government's part also feeds into the perception that it is the United States that is driving the issue, rather than Canada.

So, at the end of the day, where are we going? There are basically three things that are likely to happen. First, early warning may be the extent of cooperation. The government may say "No more." Second, the issue may be rolled into the command-and-control and operational planning issues surrounding NORAD renewal next year. NORAD will likely expand, and it is very popular. In fact, while the majority of Canadians oppose missile defense, some 60-plus percent also support Canada's joining Northern Command. So, the current dispute may very well resolve itself as the political tensions die down.

The third, and probably the worst potential outcome, is that we will negotiate to sign a framework memorandum of understanding like everyone else, which will have absolutely no value to Canada whatsoever. There remain two issues at stake: operational input and planning. The doors on NORAD have already closed to a lot of Canadian involvement. Everyone knows Canada is starting to be hurt by this. There is pressure from below to do something, but unfortunately politics stand in the way.

Finally, if we do not participate, then our strategic relationship will be seriously damaged. Canada will be further marginalized, and will end up in a continental relationship without that global picture which has been so valuable to Canadian interests.

Japan's Response to New Threats in Asia

Atsushi Ando[1]

There are several reasons why it is particularly timely to make this presentation today. Late last year, Japan made a formal decision to introduce missile defense. And last Friday, the Japanese government formally announced its new national defense strategy and five-year defense plan, which emphasizes missile defense. Furthermore, today in Tokyo, the Japan Defense Agency concluded a framework Memorandum of Understanding with the U.S. Department of Defense.

First, I would like to address the new national defense strategy and five-year defense plan. Japan initiated the review in order to adjust its defense strategy to the new global and regional security environment—an environment that is totally different from that which prevailed in 1995, when we formulated our last defense strategy.

As demonstrated by the attacks of September 11th, non-state actors—such as international terrorist organizations—have emerged as dire threats to international security. In addition to traditional dangers, such as conventional military confrontation between states, it has also become necessary for nations to address new threats, including the proliferation of weapons of mass destruction and ballistic missiles and the activities of international terrorists.

Previously, our defense capability was based upon traditional concepts of deterrence. However, traditional deterrence does not necessarily function

---

[1]Atsushi Ando is First Secretary of the political section of the Embassy of Japan to the United States. Prior to assuming this post in 2003, Mr. Ando held a series of positions at the Defense Policy Bureau of the Japanese Defense Agency, serving as deputy director of defense planning, deputy director of defense policy, and deputy director for defense intelligence.

effectively against new threats. As a result, our new defense strategy focuses on upgrading defense capabilities to be able to respond effectively to new threats, such as ballistic missile attack. The establishment of a ballistic missile defense system is one of the most important items on this agenda.

This defense review was influenced by our government's decision to introduce a missile defense system last year. This step required us to review our existing equipment and capabilities in a comprehensive manner. Japan's new defense strategy is intended to enhance our ability to deal with new threats, as well as to drastically reduce existing stocks of military equipment, which were initially intended to guard against a large-scale invasion of Japan.

Furthermore, the new national defense strategy reflects the importance of security arrangements between Japan and the United States, which continue to serve as one of the pillars of our national security. These security ties are indispensable for our national security, and the U.S. military presence in East Asia is essential for peace and safety in the region. The Japanese government is committed to enhancing Japan-U.S. security arrangements through measures such as ballistic missile defense.

In this context, BMD will have a positive and profound impact on our bilateral relations, because it will give both countries specific common goals and introduce broad areas of cooperation. BMD will contribute to making the Japan-US alliance more robust and more effective.

Second, let me detail Japan's efforts to establish our BMD system. Last December, Japan made a historic decision to move forward on deploying missile defense against ballistic missile attack. This decision was made in response to the threat posed by the growing international proliferation of ballistic missiles and weapons of mass destruction.

So far, Japan Defense Agency has invested $1 billion for 2004 on missile defense, and is currently requesting over $1 billion for 2005. The Defense Agency will acquire a near-term BMD capability by 2011, and by that point will have invested several billion U.S. dollars. In addition, the Japan Defense Agency plans to continue BMD research and analysis on longer-term BMD capabilities. In short, we have decided to make a large investment in a relatively new defense technology.

In the near term, Japan plans to take advantage of our existing equipment and facilities when we introduce the system. We will use the SPY-1 radar on Aegis ships, as well as the so-called FPS-XX radar that the Japan Defense Agency is currently developing, to detect and track ballistic missiles. To intercept missiles in the upper tier, above the atmosphere, we will use the Aegis BMD Block 04, which is now being developed by the United States. In the lower tier, we will have the Patriot/PAC 3 system to carry out interception. Since Japan already has an early version of both the Aegis and Patriot systems, the new BMD capabilities will utilize our existing infrastructure. Also, we plan to improve C2 battle management capabilities by rendering and enhancing our existing ground-based air defense system. The new BMD system will begin operation in 2007, and we will complete deployment of our near-term capability in 2011. In the longer term, Japan plans to improve our initial capability in response to evolving threats. Japan will continue research in cooperation with the U.S., specifically on advanced interceptors for the Aegis sea-based BMD system.

Thirdly, I would like to touch upon the cooperative development of operational components of the SM-3 interceptor. In this regard, it is important to discuss export control policy. Japan has been adhering to a very strict policy, the so-called "three principles," which has prohibited exports of arms even to our allies and friends. As long as we adhere to this policy, we cannot develop and produce missiles jointly with the United States. However, last Friday, when the Japanese government decided on our new national defense strategy, the chief cabinet secretary declared that in the future the "three principles" will not apply to joint development and production of a BMD system because that could contribute to the effective operation of Japan-US security arrangements, which lead to ensuring Japan's security. This is a very important step, because it paves the way for further cooperation with the United States on ballistic missile defense.

Finally, let me mention the three challenges relating to BMD that Japan currently faces.

The first is joint operations—that is, the establishment of a joint system that really works. This challenge is hardly unique to Japan; it is shared by many countries. Obviously, our defense forces have never faced a situation that required genuine joint operations over a considerable period of time. Yet because of the need for quick decision-making, timely information-sharing, and inter-service cooperation, missile defense will definitely call for such joint operations. Therefore, as an immediate goal, we would like to establish a new joint operational organization next year.

The second challenge, also operational in nature, is that of running a large and complicated BMD system in coordination with the United States. Joint operations are very difficult for our defense forces; bilateral cooperation with the United States will be even more challenging. But it is essential if we are to improve our BMD capability. It will serve as a test of the future success of military and security cooperation between Japan and the United States.

The third challenge lies in improving our large, complicated BMD system in the future. Even the United States understands that it is very difficult to develop a BMD system alone. The key to successful continuous development with limited resources is cooperation with other countries. We have cooperated closely with the United States on missile defense, including in the technical sphere, and would like to continue to do so.

We face many challenges, but these challenges could be an opportunity. Overcoming them will enhance Japan's role in international security. Japan is ready to take on these challenges, and to contribute to a safer and more stable international security environment. Missile defense constitutes a major part of this objective.

II
NEW THREATS AND CHALLENGES

Collective Defense and Coalition Solidarity

David Trachtenberg[1]

This conference comes at a particularly interesting time. We are standing on the threshold of a new spiral in the strategic environment. With the (hopefully) soon-to-be-operational missile defense capabilities that are being deployed as we speak, the United States will for the first time be able to defend all of the American people against limited ballistic missile threats.

As the recent unsuccessful test of the Ground Based Midcourse system highlights, there will be both failures and successes along the way. While failure, or the lack of success, may be frustrating and disappointing at times, we learn from our mistakes and we move forward. There is every reason to expect that is what we will do here as well.

I have been asked to address what I consider to be an interesting topic: collective defense and coalition solidarity, specifically focusing on the challenges facing the United States in maintaining alliance solidarity in the area of missile defense. It is an interesting topic because solidarity among alliance members, and among friends of the United States, has become critically important as the strategic environment has changed over the past decade or so.

During the Cold War, alliance solidarity on defense issues was in many ways relatively easy to achieve and to sustain. The Western alliance was united by the existence of an aggressive and expansionist Soviet Union, coupled with a commonly-shared belief that, in the face of the Soviet threat, solidarity was essential to the collective defense of the West. The Soviet

---

[1]David Trachtenberg is Senior Vice President for Corporate Support at National Security Research, Incorporated. Until July 2003, he served as Principal Deputy Assistant Secretary of Defense for International Security Policy at the U.S. Department of Defense.

Union was the unifying force around which collective defense structures and policies could be built. With the end of the Cold War, that unifying threat has disappeared.

In today's world, especially after the events of September 11th, maintaining alliance solidarity in the face of a more diverse suite of threats has become increasingly difficult. Yet, in this new strategic environment, missile defenses can play a critical role in both preserving and strengthening our defensive coalitions, alliances and friendships.

From the outset, the Bush administration has recognized the important linkage between missile defense and coalition security. This has been evident in speeches given by the President and senior Administration officials, as well as in strategy documents and departmental guidance that have been propagated at various levels.

The Administration has recognized that global threats—for the threat of ballistic missile attack is, in fact, a global one—require global responses. It was with this concern in mind that the commitment to cooperation with friends and allies in the area of ballistic missile defense took flight, becoming much more of a reality today than it was in the past. A lot of this momentum is also due to the fact that this administration has abandoned the Anti-Ballistic Missile Treaty of 1972, which prohibited the kind of cooperation that we are now discussing, and engaging in, with friends and allies.

There are concrete signs of this thinking. A couple of years ago, the President directed the Department of Defense to work with friends and allies on joint approaches to missile defense. This plan of action was outlined in *National Security Presidential Directive 23* (NSPD-23), which recognized that ballistic missiles pose a global threat and called for a global approach. You also can go back and look at documents like the 2002 *National Security Strategy of the United States*, which calls for the strengthening of existing alliances, the creation of new partnerships with former adversaries, and the development of effective defenses in order to defend against the use of ballistic missiles carrying weapons of mass destruction targeted either against the United States or U.S. allies. You can find similar language in the *National Strategy for Combating Weapons of Mass Destruction* issued in December 2002.

The Administration's nuclear posture, developed at the end of 2001, similarly elevated the importance of missile defense to U.S. security. The *Nuclear Posture Review* called for the development of a new triad of strategic capabilities, including missile defenses, in order to support four key defense goals and objectives. These goals are:

1) assuring allies of our commitment to their security;
2) dissuading adversaries from developing capabilities that could be used to challenge us;

deterring attacks on us or our allies and friends, and;
4) defending against and defeating any attacker should deterrence fail.

Missile defenses can and should play an important role in achieving all four of these defense goals. By forward-basing missile defenses, we can offer protection to other countries against a growing threat of ballistic missile attack. In and of itself, that act can help assure allies of our commitment to their defense. An effective, robust missile defense may also limit the potentially paralyzing effect that an adversary armed with ballistic missiles might have on our willingness to act militarily in the defense of others, friends and allies abroad. The deployment of missile defenses may also dissuade adversaries from investing scarce resources in the development of offensive ballistic missile capabilities. In large measure, the lack of missile defense capabilities to date has actually encouraged adversaries and enemies of the United States to develop those kinds of threatening offensive ballistic missile capabilities that could place us at risk.

That is not particularly surprising. We should expect to be challenged not in areas where we are superior or strong or have defenses, but in ways that exploit our greatest vulnerabilities. And ballistic missile attack has traditionally been one of our greatest areas of vulnerability.

Our ability to counter enemy missiles may even deter an attack from occurring in the first place. And of course, should deterrence fail, missile defenses can protect against the consequences of a missile attack, including against missiles carrying nuclear, biological or chemical weapons of mass destruction. Missile defenses can thus strengthen the collective security of friends and allies and make a positive contribution to collective security.

Another way to bolster coalition solidarity is to involve our friends and allies in the U.S. missile defense program. This administration has clearly sought to encourage active participation in the U.S. missile defense program. During my tenure in the Pentagon, I was involved in numerous discussions with a host of NATO allies on ways to foster international cooperation in the area of missile defense, and these efforts have been encouraging and quite productive.

That said, there are certainly those who have criticized both the Bush administration's course on missile defense and its approach to the ABM Treaty as divisive or counterproductive to alliance solidarity. In my view, however, history has proven the critics wrong. In fact, the Administration's public diplomacy efforts in laying the groundwork for a relatively smooth transition beyond the ABM Treaty and toward the deployment of an initial missile defense capability has been one of the most notable successes of President Bush's first term.

The President's missile defense policy has, without a doubt, been subjected to a healthy debate, both here and abroad. But the approach the

Administration has taken towards the debate has helped to preserve allied solidarity on the issue as well as move NATO toward a more forward-looking approach to missile defense. Missile defense, as a policy, is now a recognized and accepted feature of the post-Cold War and post-September 11th security landscape. This is a very positive development.

Some argued that the President's decision to withdraw from the ABM treaty and move forward with the deployment of missile defenses would have a negative effect on our relationship with the Russian Federation, encouraging Russian hard liners, or perhaps re-igniting an arms race and that would destroy the foundation of the new strategic relationship that the President has set out to build with Russia. Clearly, it did not, as we now know. In fact, Russia reacted relatively calmly; much more calmly than many expected. President Putin declared that the decision was not a surprise, and the U.S. approach actually did not pose a security threat to Russia.

Our allies also accepted the decision. The sun continued to rise in the east and all was generally right with the world. The ABM Treaty died with a whimper, and not with a bang, as some had expected. The President's decision to deploy missile defenses was not surprising for those that understood this President and knew where this administration was going. Alliance solidarity was not shattered.

The reason for this had much to do with the fact that the President remained absolutely firm in his commitment to remove the impediments that existed to defending the American people against ballistic missile attack, and that this commitment was repeatedly and clearly articulated to allies, Russians, adversaries and potential adversaries, and other interested parties.

In the summer of 2002, I led an interagency delegation to a number of NATO capitals to explain the Administration's position on the Treaty, on missile defenses, on what we planned to do in the absence of ABM Treaty restrictions, and also to encourage allied participation in the missile defense program for the benefit of our collective defense.

At every stop I was somewhat surprised. I had anticipated some residual commentary about the effect this might have on the Russians or the effect this might have on strategic stability or the effect this might have on some of the Cold War doctrines that had been built up and essentially accepted as gospel.

But we found all of our allies to be receptive and understanding. They all acknowledged that the world had, in fact, changed and the ABM Treaty was outdated. And they were all quite interested in learning how they might contribute, now that the Treaty's constraints on international cooperation had been removed.

In the post-ABM Treaty world, international missile defense cooperation presents the United States with an important new avenue for bolstering collective defense and Alliance solidarity. Slowly but surely, this opportunity is bearing fruit. There has certainly been significant progress made in fulfilling the President's objective of encouraging foreign participation in the missile defense program.

I won't belabor the details; I would only like to note that some very significant bilateral agreements have been concluded with a number of countries on the subject of a variety of cooperative missile defense activities.

The Administration's agreement with Great Britain to allow the upgrade of the Fylingdales earning warning radar and negotiations with Denmark for the modernization of the Thule radar facility in Greenland are both notable developments. This past summer, another framework memorandum of understanding was negotiated with Australia. The Australians are currently exploring options for equipping their Navy with the Standard Missile 3 missile defense system.

The governments of Germany, Italy, and the United States have been, and continue, working together on the MEADS system, which is seen as an anticipated successor to the Patriot missile defense system.

Cooperation with Japan is certainly impressive. Japan has indicated its intent to spend $1 billion this year, and roughly $1 billion next year, on missile defense activity. Some of the estimates I have seen indicate a willingness on the part of Japan to spend nearly $1 billion a year for the next eight or nine years.

That is a substantial financial commitment to missile defense. The Japanese are interested in both land-based and sea-based missile defense capabilities, and I was pleased to note that a memorandum of understanding has apparently been signed today formalizing some of these cooperative activities with the United States.

Japan's relaxation of the arms export ban, in place since 1976, likewise eases the way toward greater cooperation on missile defense. Cooperation with Israel is substantial and extends to assisting Israel on its Arrow missile defense program. The sharing of missile launch warning information is also involved.

There have been ongoing discussions with a number of countries, including Poland, Hungary, the Czech Republic, Taiwan, South Korea, Turkey, India, Ukraine, Canada, and a host of others, in the area of missile defense cooperation.

This is a good opportunity to engage friends, allies, and former adversaries in measures that will, in essence, help globalize a missile defense structure that will ultimately guarantee the collective security of all.

A number of Central European countries and new NATO members have expressed interest in perhaps hosting U.S. missile defense assets on their territories, something that couldn't be done under the ABM Treaty.

I would also note that the United States has actively sought to engage Russia in the area of missile defense cooperation, but with only limited success. What success we have had has been in the area of shorter-range ballistic missile defense.

There have been three joint missile defense exercises that have taken place with Russia, and there is a fourth one scheduled for next spring, which should take place in Moscow.

In 2002 and 2003, I was in charge of a U.S. delegation tasked with engaging the Russian Federation on missile defense cooperation. We met numerous times in Geneva with our Russian counterparts in an effort to explain the U.S. missile defense program and try to foster a more open and collaborative relationship in the area of missile defense.

We were extremely transparent with the Russians. We discussed a whole series of proposals and ideas for missile defense cooperation, suggesting a variety of ways we might cooperate in this area.

Progress on this front often appeared tedious and at times frustrating because it was complicated by what I would characterize as the persistence among some of certain Cold War attitudes and approaches. It was very difficult at times to convince our Russian counterparts that we were genuinely interested in cooperating with them in the area of missile defense.

We have found that, more than a decade after the end of the Cold War and the Soviet collapse, old attitudes and suspicions still die hard. Unfortunately, some of these have a tendency to cast the U.S. and our desire for missile defense cooperation in the most unfavorable of lights.

In a multilateral context, there's already a consensus within NATO to pursue missile defenses against short- to medium-range ballistic missile threats. That is good. There is currently a follow-up feasibility study that NATO is conducting to examine how missile defenses can play a role in the defense of allied populations and territories. That, I believe, is an important step that can be taken to strengthen missile defense capabilities and alliance solidarity.

The possibility of a third missile defense interceptor site, perhaps in Europe, presents a number of likely issues that will need to be addressed in order to maintain alliance solidarity.

- At least two countries have publicly indicated that any global missile defense system ought to allow other countries to have a say in the decision-making process regarding when and how that system would be used. Obviously, if all countries insist upon a role in the decision-making process as the price of their participation, the effectiveness of a

global system to counter short-time-of-flight missiles would be severely compromised.
- Another question is whether missile defense interceptors based in Europe would be used primarily to defend the United States, or to defend Europe.
- Additionally, there have been concerns raised that the intercept of a ballistic missile over populated Europe could result in debris that would rain down on Europeans, causing damage to property and death or injury to persons.

There are other political, technical and operational issues that will likely need to be resolved. Financial burden sharing is perhaps one. The export of missile defense technologies to other countries is another. As our own missile defense capabilities grow, there is a prospect that we will look to space in order to enhance the robustness of our defenses. Yet some allies are politically opposed to what they perceive as weapons in space. How will this affect their willingness to participate in a global missile defense system?

These issues are only a few of those that we will have to confront and address in dealing with alliance solidarity while improving missile defense capabilities.

It will take time and effort to make global missile defense a reality and additional challenges are bound to emerge. But if we maintain consistency in our approach and adhere to our general principles, I believe we will be able to successfully meet those challenges.

Arresting Asymmetric Proliferstion

Ilan Berman[1]

The American missile defense system we now see taking shape should not be assessed in isolation. Missile defense is intended to be a defense against attack, a particular form of attack that might be launched against the U.S. homeland, against U.S. allies, or our deployed troops.

Missile defense, however, cannot account for the spread of that technology. Missile defense is based on geography, not commerce. This became painfully clear about a year ago, when evidence began to emerge of a clandestine nuclear cartel headed by the "father" of the Pakistani nuclear bomb, Abdul Qadeer Khan.

As we have learned since, the A.Q. Khan network was far greater and more robust than originally thought. By our best estimates, it spanned more than two decades, and supplied WMD technology and know-how to a host of states, including Libya, Iran, Iraq, and North Korea.

The revelations that we have had over the last year with regard to the Khan network underscore a very frightening contemporary reality: acquisition of WMD and related ballistic missile technology is cheap and easy. This is fundamentally different than the state of affairs that prevailed during the Cold War, when proliferation was largely vertical, as states sought to make their own WMDs and ballistic missiles more sophisticated.

The vertical proliferation of the Cold War also had another distinguishing feature; it was pegged to the robustness of economies. If you were a Third World nation, you could not expect to make much independent

---

[1] Ilan Berman is Vice President for Policy at the American Foreign Policy Council, and directs the Council's work on Eurasia, transnational threats and missile defense.

headway in terms of acquiring chemical, biological, and nuclear capabilities or ballistic missiles because of economic constraints.

This is no longer the case, and the results have been predictable. Today, without exaggeration, we can say that something akin to a vibrant and self-perpetuating proliferation architecture exists. It is made up of client states like Iran and Syria, suppliers like North Korea, China, and on some occasions Russia, and secondary proliferation (as states acquire these weapons and pass them on to others).

To its credit, the Bush administration has understood this from the outset. That is why the strategy it is promoting—through such documents as the September 2002 *National Security Strategy* and the subsequent *National Strategy to Combat Weapons of Mass Destruction*—is not limited to just one initiative, such as missile defense. Rather, it is a broader, comprehensive approach designed to provide both deterrence and defense. It has evolved largely away from the public eye, but it has handed the White House some of its most significant and lasting strategic successes to date.

I'm referring, in particular, to something called the PSI, the Proliferation Security Initiative, which was unveiled by President Bush in May 2003 at the Wawel Royal Castle in Krakow, Poland. PSI is nothing less than a radical new take on nonproliferation. What it aims to do is to proactively prevent rogue states and terrorists from acquiring catastrophic capabilities through interceptions and expanded intelligence sharing agreements with nation states abroad, enhancing their legal authorities and basically creating an ad hoc arrangement that serves as a much needed law enforcement mechanism for existing arms control treaties.

This is a critical point. The PSI does not seek to create a new law, although it has in fact begun to change the parameters of contemporary international law. Rather, it seeks to modify existing law to account for bad faith actors. This is the "verify" part of the old adage "trust but verify." The idea that there could be countries acting in bad faith, and that there needs to be some way to monitor them and curb their activities if they do occur is not a parochial concern; it is one that is shared across the board in the international community. This consensus is indicated by the growing membership of the PSI.

The PSI originally had 11 core members: Australia, France, Germany, Italy, Japan, the Netherlands, Poland, Portugal, Spain, the UK and the U.S. It is now supported, in one form or another, by over 60 nations, including Russia. To put this in context, the PSI today is more than twice the size of NATO, and incorporates countries that could never be a part of that alliance.

Even though it's only a year-and-a-half old, the impact of this arrangement already has been substantial and far reaching. Through a series of interdictions and seizures in the Asia Pacific, PSI members have started to curb North Korea's proliferation activities. This is not only limited to North

Korea's missile trade, which is the DPRK's single largest source of revenue, but also extends to the regime's counterfeiting and drug trafficking activity. PSI is providing a tangible contribution to international peace and security in the Asian theater.

But even more significantly, the PSI can be credited with the decision by Libyan leader Muammar Qaddafi to make an about-face on the acquisition of WMD. The successful September 2003 interception of a German flagged ship, the *BBC China*, which was carrying nuclear centrifuges bound for the North African state, coupled with the credible threat of punitive action by the international community, convinced Tripoli that it was prudent to reverse course and give up its pursuit of nuclear and ballistic missile capabilities. This is a fantastic accomplishment. Yet it is one that by and large goes unrecognized.

Moreover, it is important to stress that the PSI is not a stand-alone effort. It is supplemented by a series of other initiatives. These include the Container Security Initiative, or CSI, which is designed to track and identify potentially hazardous cargo while it's still in foreign ports, as well as the Pentagon's "Caspian Guard" program, which is designed to beef up border security, early warning, and counterproliferation cooperation with countries in Central Asia and the Caucasus.

That is where we are with regard to the larger strategy on counterproliferation. The principal challenge, moving forward, is making sure that these mechanisms continue to be as effective as possible in stopping asymmetric proliferation, which is adapting along with changing world conditions.

Recognizing this fact, in February 2004 President Bush gave a speech before the National Defense University in which he laid out a series of new counterproliferation proposals. As part of those plans, the PSI is set to grow in scope, so that it will eventually target both WMD networks and proliferation facilitators like the A.Q. Kahn network. This is a very substantial evolution.

Of course, for this transformation to succeed, members of the PSI will have to step up their law enforcement coordination and strengthen their respective domestic legal authorities. With that in mind, the White House has invested an unprecedented sum of money, some $1 billion annually for the next ten years, to assist our allies abroad in securing their WMD supplies, and in creating internal mechanisms that make it harder to spread those technologies and those capabilities abroad.

But other priorities are clear as well. In order to be successful internationally, initiatives like the PSI have to continue to expand to include more countries. If they remain regional efforts, their effectiveness inherently will be limited.

Enlisting new members will broaden scope and reach. In this context, it is certainly a major step that we have garnered Russia's support for the PSI.

In order to move forward, we need to make a point of broadening that coalition still further. At the same time, for these efforts to be successful in the future, they will need to demonstrate their ability to adapt to new threats in new regions.

A central case is Iran. The progress Iran has made thus far on its nuclear and ballistic missile programs is clearly cause for serious concern. Just as troubling, however, is the fact that these technologies are also being spread to Iran's principal terrorist proxy, Hezbollah, as well as to countries such as Syria. Fashioning mechanisms that can adapt to these developments is critical to the success of future counterproliferation.

Clearly, our missile defense effort is going to have successes and failures. Just as clearly, the failures will be more publicized than the successes. But it is important to remember that missile defense is but one facet of a larger strategy. Counterproliferation is another. And all of these efforts are geared towards creating and maintaining American security in the face of an increasingly unpredictable, rapidly evolving, and unstable international security environment.

www.ingramcontent.com/pod-product-compliance
Lightning Source LLC
Chambersburg PA
CBHW021136300426
44113CB00006B/456